This is War

Rigby, Halley Court, Jordan Hill, Oxford, OX2 8EJ
a division of Reed Educational and Professional Publishing Ltd
www.rigbyed.co.uk

Rigby is a registered trademark of Reed Educational and Professional
Publishing Ltd

This is War first published 2002

'The Enemy Airman' © Reed Educational and Professional Publishing Ltd 2002
'We're Going to the Country' © Reed Educational and Professional
Publishing Ltd 2002
'Midsummer War' © William Bedford 2002

06 05 04 03 02
10 9 8 7 6 5 4 3 2 1

This is War   ISBN 0433 07747 6
Group Reading Pack with Teaching Notes   ISBN 0433 07753 0

Illustrated by Alexa Rutherford, Tim Clarey, David Frankland
Cover illustration © Louise Kelly / Arena 2002
Repro by Digital Imaging, Glasgow
Printed in Great Britain by Ashford Colour Press, Gosport, Hants.

The Enemy Airman

by Dennis Hamley

The Beck family, Mum, ten year-old Anna, and Paul, seven, lived in the country, not far from a great city. Mum worked on the nearby farm, doing jobs her husband once did.

Dad had joined the army when the war started. He was wounded in France and came home hobbling on a crutch. People said he was a hero. Anna and Paul hoped he would never go away again, but the doctors put him right and now he was fighting in Africa. Anna often thought of him in the Sahara desert.

Sometimes, as they walked home from school through the quiet countryside, Anna and Paul wondered how there could possibly be a war on. When darkness fell, however, they knew very well.

"Anna, will the bombers come to bomb the city tonight?" asked Paul one evening, as they opened the front gate.

"I don't know," said Anna. "They don't come every night." She looked up at the pink and blue sky and the setting sun. Soon, a full moon would rise. People called it a "bomber's moon", because the aeroplane crews could see their targets below as clearly as if it were day. Yes, they would come tonight, she thought.

"It's exciting when they come," said Paul.

"Not if you live in the city," Anna answered sharply. "Children like us are killed, or their homes destroyed, and they have nowhere to live."

"I thought they'd been evacuated to the country," said Paul.

"Some go back," explained Anna.

"Why should the aeroplanes drop bombs on children?" asked Paul.

"They don't care where they drop them," said Anna fiercely. "They think we'll get tired and frightened so we'll surrender and they can win the war. They think they can beat us but they can't!"

After supper, they listened to the radio news, hoping to hear something about the fighting in Africa. It said that a great battle was starting in the Sahara, at a place called El Alamein.

Anna and Paul slept in a room at the front of the house. Anna's bed was opposite the door and Paul's was by the window. Tonight, the sky stayed clear and, even with the curtains drawn, it was light. The moon was full and bright, like a small sun. Anna could hear chickens clucking in the back yard. Cows mooed and she heard them breathing when they came up close to the garden gate. Further away sheep bleated on the hillside behind the house, owls hooted and a vixen shrieked. Such comforting sounds usually made it easy to sleep but now, whenever she dozed off, her eyes seemed to open straight away.

Even so, she was just dropping off at last, when. . .

"Anna," Paul whispered. "Are you awake?"

"Go to sleep," she muttered.

"I can't," said Paul. "I can hear them."

At once, Anna was alert. Yes, she could hear a deep, terrible drone, far away but coming steadily nearer. Hundreds of enemy bombers were flying towards the city. She and Paul jumped out of their beds and looked through the window. Far away, the air raid siren's wail sounded. Pencils of bright light swept the sky as searchlights looked for the enemy bombers. The roar overhead grew louder.

Suddenly there were bright flashes near the city and, a few seconds later, deeper roars as anti-aircraft guns started firing. Fighters took off from nearby airfields and the sky was full of movement and noise. The fighters attacked the bombers and Anna could see the flickering lights of tracer bullets. A bomber exploded in the air. There was a blinding flash as it hit the ground some miles away.

"Hooray!" shouted Paul.

Anna thought it served them right for coming all this way just to kill. Then she thought again. There were men on that plane. Perhaps they had children waiting back home, just as she waited for Dad to come home from the war.

Most of the bombers flew on and on. Soon bright flashes of explosions and spreading fires lit up the sky as bombs dropped on the city. The raid lasted for hours. Wave after wave of bombers flew over, dropped their bombs, turned and began the long flight home. Anna and Paul could not go back to bed. They watched transfixed, and Anna felt tears silently pouring down her face. Her lovely country was being destroyed and she could do nothing about it.

Paul wasn't silent. He was beating his fists on the window and shouting, "Shoot down the lot! When I'm grown up I'll. . ."

The door opened. Mum stood there in her nightgown.

"Please be quiet, my dears," she said. "We can't do anything except pray that this awful war will soon be over."

"But Mum. . . " began Paul.

"Be quiet and go to sleep," said Mum firmly. "I have to be up early to help the farmer milk the cows, air raid or no air raid. I don't want another peep out of you."

They got back into bed, but when he heard Mum's door close, Paul scrambled back to the window again. "Anna, come here," he whispered excitedly. "Look!"

Anna's eyes followed his pointing finger. A bomber was coming down with black smoke pouring out of an engine. It descended slowly with bent and buckled propellers, shattered fuselage and smashed gun turrets. The plane seemed somehow to corkscrew in the sky as if the controls were stuck. For a dreadful second, Anna thought it would land on their house but it glided silently over and smashed into the hillside behind. The sky was a blaze of light.

"It's burning," said Paul after a few seconds. "Shall we wake Mum?"

"What can she do?" Anna replied. "Leave her alone. She needs her sleep."

Paul was looking out of the window. Once again, Anna followed his gaze.

Something else was falling out of the sky, slowly, silently, like a monstrous piece of thistledown. "A parachute," Paul breathed. "Where will he land?"

The parachute disappeared behind the house. "It's an enemy airman," said Paul. "He baled out of his plane. We should catch him and take him prisoner!"

"Don't be silly," said Anna. "Go back to bed."

For once, Paul did as he was told, but Anna knew he wouldn't be able to sleep.

Now the raid was over and silence reigned, but Anna could not sleep. Paul slipped out of bed and out of the room. When he came back, he said, "Mum's asleep."

"Good," Anna replied.

"That means we can go outside and she won't hear us," said Paul eagerly.

"You dare!" hissed Anna.

Paul was already pulling his clothes on. "If you stop me I'll wake Mum and say you're hitting me. You'll be the one who gets into trouble."

Anna did not want to wake Mum again. Besides, it would be exciting to go out and look for an enemy airman.

"Put your jersey on," she said. "It's cold outside. I'm coming too. Someone has to keep you out of trouble."

They tiptoed downstairs and out
through the back door. Soon they were
climbing the hill behind the house.

The night air struck cool, the grass
was wet, and trees were dark and
sinister. Anna shivered. Paul crept up
close. "Look," he squealed. "A ghost!"

"There's no such. . . " Anna began,
and then she saw an eerie white shape
hanging in the air.

"I told you so," Paul whimpered.

"That's no ghost," said Anna. "It's
the parachute, caught in the trees."

They heard a groan.

"Over there!" whispered Anna.

14

Fearfully, they crept towards where the groan had come from. A man wearing a leather helmet and flying jacket lay with one leg doubled up under him. He called out in words they didn't understand. He pointed to his leg and made a gesture like breaking a stick. As Anna and Paul drew nearer, the airman took his helmet off and moonlight fell on his face. Anna gasped. It was her father! He had the same face, the same hair. "Dad?" she whispered.

The man answered, but again Anna didn't understand. No, it was not her father. How could it be? Yet, just for one moment. . .

15

"We should fetch Mum," Anna said. "She'll know what to do." They ran back home. "Mum, Mum, there's a man parachuted out of a bomber," she shouted. "He's broken his leg and he's just like Dad. Come and help him."

Mum dressed quickly and ran out. When she saw the man, she too gasped. She bent down and gently tried to straighten his leg. He howled with pain and tried to say something.

"I can't understand what you're saying," said Mum in a clear voice. "My children will stay with you while I bring you coffee. It's not real but it's hot." To Anna, she said firmly, "I know he looks like Dad but he's an enemy airman. He's a prisoner of war now."

"How can he be an enemy if he looks like Dad?" said Anna.

Suddenly, out of the darkness two soldiers appeared riding motor cycles, followed by a fire engine, a lorry with a crane and trailer, a large car and an army ambulance with a big red cross on it.

The airman felt inside his jacket and took out a photograph. Two children – a girl and boy. Anna smiled and squeezed his hand, even though he was an enemy. Two soldiers jumped from the ambulance with a stretcher. Mum brought the coffee, which the airman drank gratefully.

Then a stern-looking man in a black overcoat stepped from the car. He waited while the airman was placed on the stretcher and then he spoke to him. The airman understood and nodded.

The wreckage was loaded onto the trailer. One wing showed the badge of the RAF. An ambulance man said, "A British Lancaster. The metal will be melted down and next month it will fly again, as a Messerschmitt." The procession drove away. Anna, Paul and Mum were alone.

"Will he be all right?" asked Anna.

"I hope so," said Mum. She looked grave. "The man in the overcoat was Gestapo."

That night, they listened to the news,
hoping to hear more about El Alamein.
There was nothing. Later they heard that
Rommel's Afrika Korps had been
defeated by the British Eighth Army, and
many prisoners were taken.

Months passed before they heard,
through the Red Cross, that Dad was
safe, a prisoner of war in England.
Always, when Anna thought about
the enemy airman who looked
like her father's double, she
felt as if her father had
come that morning to
tell her he was a
prisoner of war
as well.

"Samuel Clegg! Will you sit still and stop fidgeting!" Mr Horner's voice cut through the steady rhythm of the steam train.

"My label's come off, Sir, and I can't find my gas mask!"

"It's under your seat, boy, where you put it. Why can't you keep it round your neck like everyone else?"

"I'm sorry, Sir. I'm just a bit excited. I've never been on a train before."

"Neither have most of the other children, Samuel, but they're not climbing all over it like monkeys, are they? Just settle down now!"

The day had started early. Mrs Clegg had delivered Sam and his younger sister, Hannah, to school for eight-thirty. Mrs Clegg had tried to remain calm. As she walked away from the school gates, she turned once to see Sam waving wildly. Hannah was just standing there, clutching her brown teddy with the chewed ear. Mrs Clegg burst into tears.

"We're being evacuated," explained Sam, as his sister wiped away two large tears from her own eyes. "We're going to the country, Hannah. What fun!"

"I don't want to be evacuated," said Hannah, "and neither does teddy! I want to stay at home with Mummy. I don't like the country."

"Well, you can't stay at home. It's too dangerous. Mummy doesn't want us at home when the bombs start falling."

They had set off for the railway station just after morning playtime. It was only a short distance from school and the children had walked, marching in a double line like soldiers. They had brown name labels tied to their coats, and gas masks in cardboard boxes hanging loosely by their sides.

The platform was noisy and crowded. There were children everywhere, spilling out of their lines to peer down the track, ask questions, or to visit the station toilet.

Hannah was crying quietly to herself, confused and alone. Sam could see her further down the platform, but he couldn't get to her. He was with his own class and, besides, he was enjoying the bustle and confusion.

The train was late. Its arrival was announced by a single, long blast on the whistle. As it pulled into the station, clouds of steam billowed and hissed across the platform. The children squealed and screamed and leaped backwards out of the way.

The guard strode along the platform shouting, "Stand back! Stand back!" He flung open the doors, so that they crashed back against the carriages. The children were on board within minutes, and excited faces peered from the windows. They waved frantically at everyone in sight, as the grumpy guard banged the doors shut and signalled for the journey to commence.

"Are we nearly there, Sir?" enquired Sam, excitedly. He was kneeling up on the seat with his face pressed against the window.

"We've only been travelling for twenty-five minutes, Samuel. We've barely left London."

"How long will it take, Sir? To get to the country, I mean? I can't wait!"

"My mother said it would take at least three and a half hours," put in Harold Spink. He was sitting on the opposite side of the carriage to Sam, peering at him over the copy of *Just William* he had brought to read.

Sam glared at him and repeated the question.

"About three and a half hours," confirmed Mr Horner. "Now do sit down, Samuel, and give us all some peace."

Sam sank back into his seat and glared again at Harold, who had a smug smile on his face, as if to say, "I told you so."

The train clattered on relentlessly.

Gradually, the rows of red-brick houses
and smoky factory chimneys thinned
and gave way, first to rough scrubland
and then to green fields.

Sam was fascinated. He had never been
out of London before. The only big
stretch of grass he had ever seen was in
the local park. He used to go there every
Saturday morning with his dad. They
would play football and visit the boating
lake. That was before the war. Now his
dad had gone away, and he
had not heard from him
for over two months.
He stared out of the
train window at the
lush, green fields
and thought how
much he missed
him.

A thin drizzle had started to fall from a grey sky that seemed to be getting ever closer to the ground. The droplets stuck to the carriage window and the speed of the train blew them into shapes and patterns. Sam traced the shapes with his finger on the inside of the window. Mr Horner had his eyes closed. His mouth fell open and he began to snore gently.

Suddenly, Sam let out an excited yell and jumped to his feet. Mr Horner jerked forward and almost fell off his seat. Harold dropped his book in fright.

"What is it, Samuel? What on Earth's the matter?"

"It's cows, Sir! I've spotted some cows in a field!"

"Cows!" exclaimed Mr Horner. "I thought you'd spotted Adolf Hitler himself, the way you exploded!"

"I've never seen cows before, Sir. I didn't realise they were so big."

"Yes, well, they're very nice, cows," said Mr Horner, putting his hand on his heart. "Now sit back down, will you, Samuel."

Harold shook his head and recovered his book from the floor.

Three hours went by. Two coaches further along the train, Hannah had stopped crying and was staring in wonder out of the carriage window, as the countryside unfolded before her eyes.

In his compartment, Sam was asleep. Mr Horner was sitting opposite him, looking a little happier. The teacher had thought seriously about waking Sam up, but had changed his mind. It was so restful without Sam's non-stop chatter. However, the train was slowing and the station was in sight.

"Wake up, lad! We've arrived! Time to get your things together!"

Sam pulled himself upright and stared in confusion around the carriage. Harold put his book carefully into his satchel.

"Where are we?" muttered Sam. "Why is the train stopping?"

"We've arrived, lad," repeated the teacher.

Sam shook his head and yawned.

There was a screech of brakes as the train pulled slowly towards the small platform, before stopping with a sudden jerk. Sam felt nervous, without knowing quite why.

"Make sure you've got everything," instructed the teacher. "You'll have to do without anything you leave on board."

Mr Horner pulled down the carriage window, leaned out, and twisted the handle to open the door.

"Out you come," he said. "Go and stand across the platform, near to those wooden seats."

Sam stepped down onto the platform.
He shivered as the cold air hit him.

"Samuel Clegg! I think you've forgotten
something!"

Sam turned to see Mr Horner holding
his suitcase. "Thanks, Sir," said Sam, and
he took the case from the teacher.

Hannah ran up to Sam with a beaming
smile on her face. She was much happier
now.

"Wasn't the train journey fun!"

"It was all right," said Sam, quietly.

He glanced nervously up and down the
platform, feeling uncomfortable in these
strange, new surroundings.

The next half hour was confusing. The
small platform overflowed with children.
Several ladies sat at a long trestle table at
the far end of the platform. A stern-
looking policeman stood to one side.

Mr Horner called for quiet, and the childish voices on the platform hushed.

"I want you all to listen carefully," said Mr Horner. "This is Mr Pollard, your billeting officer." He pointed to a tall gentleman, who wore a long, grey coat and had a pair of wire-rimmed spectacles perched on the end of his nose. "When Mr Pollard calls you forward, you must walk to the table. That is where you will be introduced to your host. Are there any questions?"

There were none, and Mr Pollard began calling out names.

"I don't want to stay with a ghost!" said Hannah.

"It's HOST," corrected Sam. "We're all going to stay with host families, until it's safe to go back home."

"Are we going home now, Sam?" asked Hannah, quietly.

"No, we're not going home yet," said Sam, putting an arm around her, more for his own comfort than for hers.

"Samuel and Hannah Clegg!" shouted the billeting officer.

Sam was so nervous that he couldn't move. He stood rooted to the spot beside his suitcase.

"Come on," said Hannah, pushing him forward. "We're going to meet our ghost!"

"Samuel and Hannah Clegg?" enquired one of the ladies. Sam nodded.

"You're with Mr and Mrs Hughes at Stone Farm. You are lucky! You'll be able to help out on the farm. And they've got a boy about the same age as you, Samuel.

Why – here's Mrs Hughes, now."

Sam glanced up and felt a sense of pure relief. Mrs Hughes had a warm, welcoming smile.

"So you're my new children," she said. "My word, you're a bit scrawny! Don't worry, we'll soon feed you up! Let's get you home."

She took hold of Hannah's hand, and they all walked off across the platform.

"SAMUEL CLEGG!" bellowed Mr Horner's weary voice. "You've left your case behind again, lad!"

THE MIDSUMMER WAR
by William Bedford

I could hear the wireless chattering in the kitchen and then my mum shouting for Grandpa in the yard. Grandpa was good at disappearing, especially when there were jobs that needed to be done. It drove her mad.

This afternoon he was supposed to be tidying the cellar. I tried to concentrate on my Meccano but Mum was pounding up the stairs, shouting "Philip!" as if there was a fire, and I knew it was hopeless. I was building a Meccano frigate. It was the most difficult model I'd done, as the screws were so hard to fit.

Mum burst into my room. "He's gone!" she said, grabbing hold of my arm. "His bike's gone out the shed. I knew he'd do something like this."

"Hang on, Mum!" I tried to protest, but I was soon following her down the narrow stairs and out into the back yard. The shed door was wide open. She was right. Grandpa's bicycle had gone.

"He's gone fishing," she said angrily, pushing her untidy hair back out of her eyes. "I've told him time and again he should stay near the house. It's too dangerous."

"I'll soon find him," I said, wheeling my own bike out into the lane behind the houses.

"You just be careful," she shouted, as I turned the corner.

I didn't tell her what I had noticed in the shed. Something had been taken that told me exactly where Grandpa had gone in his bid for freedom. He hated being trapped in town by the constant air raids. He felt it was like being in prison and sometimes I did, too.

I cycled along the cobbled lane that runs behind the fish docks. The buildings along the quay had suffered a lot of bomb damage. One of them, Smethurst's ice house, had been bombed a week ago and was still smouldering.

Beyond the quays, the lane turned down to the promenade. The sea was a deep blue, reflecting the cloudless summer sky. Out on the river, there was a trawler, slowly moving towards the port.

Dad had worked on one of these before he joined the navy. Now these old trawlers were used as minesweepers because hundreds of mines had been dropped in the river since the beginning of the war.

I felt the salt wind blowing in my face and suddenly I, too, was free. It was almost as if I'd woken up. I waved to the rusty vessel and cycled hard towards the creeks where I knew I would find Grandpa. They were about three miles beyond the town. When the tide was out, flounders and plaice hid in the shallow, muddy waters. The little inshore fishing vessels moored there when they weren't working. It was Grandpa's favourite fishing place.

I saw him immediately. He was wading in the shallow waters of the creek, with the spear he had taken from the shed in his hand. It was an old broom handle with a sharp knife tied to the end. I dropped my bike in the sand dunes and watched.

Grandpa was motionless in the water. Herring gulls screamed and wheeled over his head. Suddenly, his arm darted down and the spear came up with a big fat flounder threshing on the end.

"Got you!" Grandpa shouted in his excitement.

He turned briskly to wade out of the creek but halted when he saw me. "She sent you after me!" he said, glaring at the fish still threshing on the end of the spear.

I shrugged. "I fancied a bit of fishing," I told him.

He grinned. "Oh aye," he said sceptically. "Pull the other one, Philip."

"She's worried," I said as he climbed out of the creek and dropped the fish into his collecting bag. "You know what she's like."

Grandpa frowned. "I just need a bit of peace, Phil. If I can't go fishing, Hitler's already won."

"He'll win even quicker if you get blown up," I pointed out, but Grandpa wasn't listening. "How about getting some more fish for supper?" he said with a big grin, offering me the spear.

It was late afternoon when I saw the wild geese over the North Sea – only they weren't birds. They were flying in rigid formation, droning out of the east. To the west, over the hills behind us, the sun was going slowly down. As the tide turned, the moored fishing vessels bobbed gently against the waves.

"Stukas," Grandpa said quietly, the fishing spear forgotten in his hands. The Stukas turned towards the crowded estuary.

"They're heading for the docks."

Shell bursts floated above the helpless vessels. The guns on the mainland returned their fire.

I saw one of the Stukas dive through the shell bursts and then lift away, like a deadly cormorant. The bomb curved down towards the sea and landed with a splash of white water. After a long silence, the bomb exploded, the sound drifting across the estuary. They were heading up the river now. We could hear the sirens wailing, down by the docks. Another plane from the formation broke off and dived towards the sea. It was going for one of the minesweepers. A high-pitched whistling scream filled the air, like a boiling kettle gone mad, then the bomb exploded in the water. The minesweeper fired back after the retreating Stuka.

"Kill 'em!" Grandpa was yelling, jumping up and down in the water of the creek, soaking both of us in his excitement. "Let 'em have it, boys!"

I was thinking about Mum. She was terrified of the raids, though she refused to show it. She would be frantic, wondering what had happened to us.

The guns were still firing and the sirens were still wailing. It was like a huge firework display, taking place over the docks and the narrow terraces where we lived.

"What about Mum?" I said, watching the fight over the river. "We ought to go and find Mum."

"She'll be all right," Grandpa said, squeezing my arm. He bent forward, forgetting his excitement for the moment. "She'll be down the shelter, don't you worry."

Ack-ack guns were stuttering all along the coast now, the air vibrating with their relentless firing. Against the dark sky in the east, long streams of tracer shells climbed, yellow and red, slowly into the sky. Great swathes of blue light searched the sky over the sea.

We climbed to the top of one of the dunes to get a better view as the sun sank to the west. Suddenly, I heard a movement behind us.

"Listen," I whispered. Grandpa peered into the gathering darkness. We would be in real trouble if it was the coast guards or the army. They might think we were German spies.

"I knew you'd be here," a voice hissed from the darkness. Then we saw her emerging from the dunes.

"Mum!"

"You ought to know better, you two," she said. "This is no place to be when there is a raid on."

"Jerry isn't going to keep me locked up," Grandpa said.

There was a sudden roar overhead and we all spun round. Coming from inland, out of the sinking sun, were Spitfires, heading for the estuary. I yelled with delight. Grandpa jumped up and down, cheering. The Spitfires flew out of the sun and straight for the town. The guns were firing all the time, splitting the air, bright lights burning the evening sky. It was like a mighty thunderstorm. At my side, Mum pressed her hands against her mouth as she stared wide-eyed at the battle.

There were dogfights going on all down the river now. The Stukas were trying to break free and make for the open sea but Spitfires seemed to be coming from everywhere. Another Stuka spun out of the sky in a plume of smoke and disappeared into the freezing waters of the North Sea.

The minesweepers and the coastal guns thumped the summer air.

Suddenly a Stuka was caught in the beams of two searchlights. It zoomed and dived to escape but the lights clung on. Then every gun along the shores and estuary opened fire. Blinding flashes ripped the sea. A blaze of searchlights hung on to the enemy plane.

The Stuka dived and spiralled, and suddenly it hurtled along the coast towards us. The searchlights held it in a blaze of light. The plane looped through the light and we could hear the engines now. More guns fired, and then suddenly the Stuka became a shooting blaze of yellow, trailing through the sky towards the water.

"It's going to crash!" Grandpa shouted.

We flung ourselves down to the ground. My mouth was full of sand. I could feel my mother's arm round my shoulder. There was a burst of blue light and then a hiss as the Stuka hit the sea.

Lifting our heads slowly, we crawled up to the top of the dune and watched the dying plane. It had landed right in the middle of the deserted fishing boats. Flames hissed and flared. Blue sparks flew in the air. The boats burned fiercely, their wooden hulks and sails crackled with flames.

Then there was a thud and another burst of flame. The Stuka exploded, disappearing beneath the water. The crew didn't stand a chance. There was nothing left. We stood in silence. All the excitement had gone. Quietly, Grandpa took his cap off, and ruffled his hair. I could see the tears shining on my mother's cheeks.

We stood watching the raid for over an hour until the air-raid sirens took up their eerie cry again, sounding the "all clear". Searchlights were still trying to pierce the clouds of red smoke above the town but the Stukas had all gone. The guns stopped firing.

"We showed 'em," Grandpa said, but his voice sounded tired, weary.

"This time," Mum said quietly.

We packed the fishing gear and the flounders we'd caught, and wheeled our bicycles up onto the narrow coast road. I could hear the siren of an approaching fire engine.

"Better get home and see what damage they've done," Mum said, trying to sound cheerful.

"Long as we can go fishing, the Germans haven't won," Grandpa said.

"That's right," Mum said, with a quiet smile. I knew she was thinking about Dad. So was I.

We went home and got on with the War.